Memo on

Big

Oil

and the

Taxes They (Don't) Pay

Michael Bindner

Bindner Analytics

Center for Fiscal Equity

© 2019, Michael Bindner

ISBN: 9781097350568

Imprint: Independently published

Nonfiction > Business & Economics > Industries > Energy

Nonfiction > Business & Economics > Taxation > Corporate

Table of Contents

Forward

Why should we bother with an analysis of Big Oil and the taxes they pay (or don't pay)? Is there any hope in changing the status quo, or is the TINA correct, that there is no other way? If we don't examine the question, we will never know.

Robert Reich posted the now familiar figures on May 5, 2019 about how much Exxon Mobil and other oil companies pay (or rather do not pay) in corporate income taxes. What he writes is absolutely true from a cash basis because current year taxes are reduced by past accrued losses. This actually is reasonable from an accounting view point.

Companies operate on an accrual basis, so tax payment should match their accounting system. It seems TINA is correct, or is it. It depends upon your point of view. We are never going to force Big Oil or Big Business to abandon an accounting system that works for us as well.

Economists, particularly Marxists, look at additional perspectives. When we do so, we can explore how things really work (what the powers that be do not want you to know) and how things can be done differently (what they really, really, really don't want you to know). There Is a Better Alternative after all (TIBA).

Oil companies are both a government agency that provides oil and a massive cooperative which also employs teachers, clergy, farmers, food processors, builders, bankers, etc. Either viewpoint is a social or socialistic accounting of their activities. Both viewpoints reflect decisions made in both the public sector and by management. The value in this analysis is to lay bare these decisions and explore options.

Paying Taxes

Big Oil, as an enterprise, actually pays a massive amount in taxes locally, nationally and internationally. It depends on how you count.

Accounting rules have a libertarian bias. Libertarians see all activities as discrete purchases, but are they really? The wage that is paid must include a net pay that, while not set by perfect competition (see below), they must be adjusted by the amount of taxation imposed by the government. Employees care much more about what they take home than their total wage, except as a measure of comparison with others and at tax time.

Oil oligopolists, or their sub-units, write checks for taxes on payroll, fuel, extraction and income for employees, subsidiaries, contractors and franchisees. Also, health care, which in all other OECD countries is paid by taxes, can be imputed as public revenue.

Employees also pay sales and property taxes and receive tax credits. Put another way, these taxes pay for all the private and public consumption of their employees, retirees and investors.

Property taxes are paid by wealthier individuals, both occupants and landlords, however landlords derive money from rent to pay these taxes. Sales taxes are regressive

8

and state income taxes are mostly proportional, but both must be paid from wages that come through their employees with each gallon of gas consumed.

Oil companies fund government through their workers. All government comes through either taxation of the corporation and individuals or by public borrowing. This includes bonds as a portion of employee sponsored benefits and 401(k) retirement savings. Both taxes and benefits are the result of political decision making.

Political decisions are assumed to be an egalitarian exercise by the citizens through the ballot box, while company decisions are made by company executives and management, with a nod to the wishes of investors through a board of directors that is mostly made up of members suggested by management. Oil companies influence government decisions in a big way as well (this is before you consider the revolving door between corporate and governmental employment).

While federal gas and income taxes are universal, who pays them is the result of company decision-making as well as consumer preference. Companies do not drill or process oil in the same places. When consumers buy gas, they send their money to some places and not others, both foreign and domestic, based on the supply and distribution decisions made by the companies from which they buy gas. A factor involved in those decisions, aside from necessity, is tax policy – the largest local tax expenditure being education.

The largest income transfer for many employees and their families before retirement age is education. A family with a large number of children often receives more in education spending than on cash income. Because education is mandatory, it is also an entitlement.

Other spending benefits some, but not others. All transportation spending, from air travel to motor vehicles and roads, benefit the oil industry directly. One of the largest supply costs for the Air Force is Avgas. Public land activities, including Indian Affairs which serves as a buffer between the tribes and the oil companies, benefits the oil companies. Energy Department activities have slowed research on Fusion to a crawl, when it should be accelerated. If you count the White House as a captured agency and Putin as an oil company, there is nothing that is not touched.

Royalty payments are both a tax determined by governments and a purchase, as revenue is often used to influence elections in the developed world and buy friendly governments in the developing world. Such activities border on corruption and in the view of many, cross those borders at the expense of voters at home and abroad. To make sure all runs smoothly, oil companies insist on strong defense spending.

Defense Spending

Defense spending eats a majority of discretionary funds. While Defense employment can rescue young people from poverty, in exchange for risking life and limb, they do so as much to defend American interest as protect the homeland. Sometimes, this is blatant, as when the working title for the second Gulf War (which is still with us) was called Operation Iraqi Liberation. This kind of gave it away and was quickly changed. Luckily for us, the word got out.

Department	Component	Subtotal	Department	Total
Defense				750
Air Force (sub/all)		84	166	
AF MILPERS	37			
AF O&M-Civ+MILCON	47			
Army (sub/all)		66	182	
Army MILPERS	57			
Army O&M-Civ+MILCON	9			
Navy (sub/all)		88	206	
Navy MILPERS	34			
Marine MILPERS	16			
Nav O&M-Civ+MILCON	30			
Mar O&M-Civ+MILCON	8			
O&M Civilian Pay (Ar,AF,N)		60		
Procurement (all DoD)		117		
Aircraft	39			
Ships	24			
Other Procurement	54			
RDT&E (all services)		104		
War (inc. pay all services)		58		
DoD Other		143	196	
DoD O&M (inc. Civilian Pay)	72			
DoD Agencies + Hidden	71			
Human Service				300
Education			62	
Housing & Urban			44	
Human Services			90	
Labor			11	
Veterans Affairs			93	
Safety				137
Homeland Security			52	
Justice			29	
State & International			43	
Treasury			13	
Science				99
Agriculture			21	
Commerce			12	
Energy			32	
Interior			13	
Transportation			21	

This table illustrates how much Defense (and Big Oil) own the government. Even components of the DoD are bigger than most departments. It is no accident that the Department of Veterans Affairs needs the largest budget of all other departments. While veterans have better access to government jobs, they also need access to government health care for service-related injury. These decisions take longer to make, on average than the final decision to get us into war.

The biggest beneficiaries, aside from Big Oil, are defense contract workers and shareholders. Overall, they are a more highly paid workforce and investment than the economy at large.

Defense contractor CEO salaries are capped at $1 million per year in allowable cost, but additional salary and benefits can be distributed out of fee payments over allowed costs. CEOs are also given stock incentives, so that when the company does good, they do good. CEOs sometimes create crises then solve them to make their improvements look better than they are. This is not good if you are in the field and the crisis is your possible demise.

Entitlements

The biggest item that Big Oil must pay is social insurance. Luckily for the majority of citizens, progressive or progressive looking coalitions assure benefits, provided that they placate economic elites. These employee and employer-paid benefits are primarily for social security and health care systems that benefit the entire population (even the low income and no income poor). Employers write the actual checks. Marx fully supported social insurance, as do most capitalists. Both acknowledge that it both benefits workers and creates a better cage. Without it, workers tend to get restless, as they during the Great Depression.

It took the threat of socialism by Franklin Delano Roosevelt to get capitalist buy-in for both enhanced labor protections and passage of Social Security. Reactionaries have been trying to claw both back for decades.

Libertarians would end most of the social benefit programs for individuals. They do not like the better cage concept. They assume that private incentives would have workers demand adequate income and the necessary savings to escape poverty, if they were only relieved of the obligation to pay taxes. This sounds good for the upper-middle class, but almost of half the population have insufficient income to make up for government services lost, from parents to retirees.

Big Oil's useful libertarians hope that the pain of transition away from social benefit to private savings might create the existential crisis that brings about liberty. Revolutions, however, bring about suffering. Marxists tried to take advantage of crisis in Russia and got Oligarchs, both before and after the Soviet state fell. The Great Recession of 2008 was one of those tipping points that they think should have brought about Libertopia. It did not.

The reality of social benefits would make poor families responsible, as they once were, for their retired seniors, giving a subsidy to workers whose parents had the decency to die already and without medical bills or to have large families who can take care of the burden. Many cannot. It is why we have social insurance.

Social Insurance taxes pay out enough of a benefit to retirees to help fend of starvation, paying lower income workers more than they would earn in the private market with the same investment (which is why the wealthy fund efforts to privatize retirement funding). This partially makes up for an economic system with an uneven income distribution. Some tax benefits, like the EITC which is a kick back of payroll taxes and other income transfers go to lower income individuals, while higher taxes for wealthier individuals make tax expenditures, such as mortage interest, benefit wealthier taxpayers whose tax benefits exceed the standard deduction.

Social Security has been prefunded, so that workers subsidized tax cuts promised to higher income taxpayers by President Reagan, both of which were paid by employers or dividend payers (save for capital gains, which come from gambling on asset values). The debt to save the Reagan tax cuts is now coming due and can only be paid by or borrowed from income tax payers (which, again, are primarily paid through their employers or through dividends paid).

In all cases, the money to pay these taxes comes from the end consumer, through the employing company to the government. The employee never sees it, as it should be. If the employee did have the option, he or she would never pay it. That is why only the upper middle class have any significant retirement savings from voluntary savings programs.

When the Soviet Union fell, state owned enterprises distributed shares to employees. I suggested how to go about this to President Yeltsin's U.S. advisors. The problem was that the financial sector insisted that these shares be immediately tradeable. Currently, they are held by oligarchs and are worth a lot of money. When they were distributed, they were valued as penny stocks. Workers sold them to buy food or vodka. They did not see that the power of wealth is not the money, it is the ability to control decision making over your own future.

Health care benefits take a significant sum of any enterprise, especially if you include subsidies for retirees (which are not income-based until non-covered expenses exceed assets) and the health care exclusion on corporate income taxes. If health insurance is considered as revenue for comparison purposes with other developed nations, then according to Bruce Bartlett, the United States public sector is 43% of the economy.

If you count households rather than the amount of income, more than half are dependent on government for their income – and that is before you count the health sector. A past president of General Motors used to state that he ran a health care company that made cars. That obligation was lessened by restructuring which gave the union a non-voting ownership share to maintain benefits but required agreement to a two-tier system that gave lower pay and benefits to newly hired employees.

In 2005, President Bush convened a Tax Reform Panel. Even with a progressive income tax included in the calculations, I calculated that an inclusive consumption tax funding current spending would amount to about 46%.

All of these decisions are determined by voters, however, the rich have a thumb on the scales.

Tax Cuts, Big Oil & 2008

The important starting point is that most taxes that went up and down are collected by employers on behalf of their employees, who reconcile their tax burden every spring. Their refunds clean their cage annually, although for the poorest, the tax preparers get a sizeable fee for their cleaning services. Only taxes on capital gains are not collected through employers. Like their vandguardist Donald Trump, they cheat.

2008 was caused by the tax reform in 1986, when reform encouraged home owners to turn their mortgages into automatic teller machines that would be refilled on sale. It was also the part of a move to control inflation through giving the CEO class an incentive to cut worker pay, benefits and union rights (helped by the government) by decreasing their marginal tax rates. High marginal rates used to seize any gains that went to the CEO for cost cutting, but the Kennedy-Johnson cuts which took effect in the mid-1960s started a roll back in marginal rates from 91% at the top to 28% in 1986.

Bush 42 rationalized tax rates in a way that raised taxes on billionaires to 31%, but gave us a system that was mostly proportional at that rate when the phase out of Payroll Taxes are included. while Clinton delayed what Michael Harrington thought was an inevitable crisis by increasing tax rates on the wealthiest, which balanced the budget, increased spending and helped clean the cage.

Clinton started fouling the cage by making a deal with the devil (Gingrich) to lower capital gains tax rates, bring about the tech boom and the related recession. He also followed the advice of Uber Neo-Lib Larry Summers in repealing Glass-Stiegel and leaving hedge funds unregulated.

In 2001, Bush 44 doubled down with more cuts (originally to preserve the availability of debt capital for the Federal Reserve to use for currency arbitrage, but later to recover from the recession). The reality is that he started fouling the cage by cutting marginal rates to put more money back into the asset markets. He doubled down two years later by decreasing capital gains and dividend tax rates, which benefit the rich and asset speculators and no one else.

Asset markets have zero to do with causing economic growth, which is defined as increase in government spending, government worker, retiree and beneficiary consumption and second order consumption in the private sector, with third order investment resulting from consumption and funded through primary, not secondary, asset markets. Supply-side is a myth by Austrian economists who fuel booms that create busts so that new firms might emerge, damn the hindmost and their employees who feel the pain of such Financial Darwinism.

The fundamentals were so bad in Y2K that massive infusions of credit were added so that consumers could borrow, covering the bets that asset investors made on garbage investment products, leaving many borrowers with junk mortgages and everyone else extracting money from the ATM scheme in the 1986 Tax Reform.

The run-up to the crisis had everything to do with Big Oil. Before the crisis, the New York Mercantile Exchange was largely unregulated. Futures contracts were bid higher and higher. While this helped bring about a scramble of exploration and research, the fundamentals of supply and demand did not match the market. Congress enacted a law that limited speculation and the price crashed. To cover their bets, they tried to liquidate mortgage backed securities. We know how that went.

Libertarian Republicans tried to block the relief package (which should have gone to borrowers, but did not), crashing the stock market and assuring the election of Barack Obama, who brought in the usual neo-liberals, including Summers, who with Ben Bernanke saved the financial sector and did nothing for underwater borrowers, including this author and his family.

No revolution occurred. Instead, Obama kept the Bush 44 tax cuts in place, prolonging the recovery of asset markets and doing nothing for the economy at large. After the tax cuts on the looked wealthy were repealed, (leaving the upper-middle class with their tax cuts), an anemic recovery resulted. The Trump tax cuts were an attempt to bring back asset speculation, but the Orwellian sounding *Balanced Budget Act of 2018* did nothing of the kind. It increased spending (finally) and the economy is now in recovery. Sadly, Trump is claiming credit.

Governments which borrow money rely on the good will of property owners to service local debt and bond purchasers for both municipal and national debt finance, with the interest serving as a subsidy for bond holders. Debt is high enough that paying it back is a multi-year project, and that is when you recognize that the ability to pay it back is dependent on the income taxes paid. Income tax payers owe $13 for every dollar of taxes paid in a year. Debt owed then becomes a function of income distribution. Those who pay nothing, owe nothing. Put another way, the top 1% of income owe $7 Trillion of our $19 Trillion Debt. While a good deal of that income comes from gambling on assets, a large percentage will be paid back from executive level compensation through salaries and dividends. These are paid for through the company by those who pay for gas.

Taxes and Voting

Tax rates and bases are set through a variety of social factors. Ideally, office holders who impose these taxes are elected on an equal vote basis (though some classes of workers cannot vote, including ex-convicts and children and the victims of voter suppression).

According to Anthony Downs in his Theory of Non-voting, no one voter has hope of deciding the election (tell that to Madam President Clinton) because, while we can determine how close any single voter is to the views of the candidate, dividing these factors by the size of the population makes voting a fool's errand. Down's equation is unbalanced, however. He ignores the influence of political parties in decisions to vote. A well-run campaign always gives the impression so that the election is close, even when there is no way the opposition or candidate can win. While there are clues in the news and in normal discourse to validate these claims, they are usually fairly accurate.

Within a party, candidates fear the influence of organized factions, like the Tea Party, pro-life Catholics and Evangelicals and Make America Great Again on one side and teachers' unions on the other (minority voters are mostly assumed to be loyal, although miscalculation on Catholic and Black Male voters cost Hillary the White House). This enforces party orthodoxy. In proportional systems, such factions can be shunted to minor parties, which guarantees that no vote is wasted because the final coalition may or may not include their party. Everyone votes in Puerto Rico, which has this system, but every Puerto Rican on the mainland does not vote.

Fundraising is a huge factor in getting the word out. In single-member districts and on most policy issues, there is enough heterodoxy among the entire universe of voters, including in the office holder's party, to allow the candidate to take money from and grant access to a variety of interests. This allows the donor class, including corporations like Exxon Mobil, with a free speech right, an outsize influence in having both access to elected officials and an influence over the voters themselves. The secret ballot and loosely organized parties allow some measure of freedom, with more informed voters having more freedom and less informed voters being more vulnerable to advertised viewpoints.

Partisan competition for donors puts a finger on the scale when determining taxes.

This is why true socialism has been voted into office. Even in socialistic countries, monopolistic elites exercise despotic control over the political process and bring politics into the economy to such an extent that it functions more for the benefit of the elite than for everyone else.

In short, oil companies have a great deal of control over what they spend in the public sector. This is one type of socialism. Government tax and spending benefits are weighted away from the poor to the middle class. Wages have either greater inequality.

Being Owned

There is another type of virtual socialism that requires, or should require, a living wage for employees. When a company buys a person, they should bear the cost of maintaining the needs of that person, sometimes inadequately (especially at the final distribution point), sometimes adequately and sometimes excessively, based on what is seen as the market value of the services provided by the employees in a market that can be characterized as competitive monopsony.

Monopsonist labor markets have fewer buyers than sellers, giving the buyers an advantage in all negotiations. Worse, some markets are oligopolistic or fully monopsonist, especially when government service or contracting is involved – of course, in those cases the other side of the market is competitive monopoly because the barriers to entry are balanced out by the customization of the product.

The mix of these factors yields higher wages, but work conditions and wages are not what they would be if sellers and buyers were on an equal footing – such as representation by a union with a collective bargaining agreement.

Monopsonist labor markets lead to hierarchical organizational structures and despotic management styles. There is absolutely no room for free expression. You work, dress and speak at the whim of the employer. They call this professionalism, but real professionals are not treated like children.

The situation for the non-professional and non-unionized working class is even worse. Low wage employees really are treated like children. They often do not have the skills beyond high school level, if that, and if they are graduates of workforce development programs designed to remove families from welfare, they are often trained to be servants for both the rich and the poor in hospitals and nursing homes.

Many of the working poor are in jobs where they work with high school and college students. If they are lucky, the student workers are covered through some kind of insurance through their parents. If not, they may have government benefits. Older workers who labor side-by-side with student workers and get exactly the same benefits – none except for maybe free food or free movies.

Immigrants have it the worst. Highly skilled workers are brought in by countrymen in the tech field, nurses are given residency while causing a nursing shortage back home and students with visas get H-1B status without quotas. Agricultural workers get in on H-2A visas, but have no path to residency. In either case, if the sponsoring employer does not like anything about the visa holder, from performance to attitude, they are deported.

Undocumented workers can find work in food service and be treated with some respect. Asylees and legal immigrants are often not allowed to practice their professions due to re-credentialing requirements and end up starting a small business or work in a family business or one by a fellow immigrant (although some fellow immigrants and diplomatic personnel treat their workers as slaves, especially in the household sector).

Foreign nationals are brought in by Coyotes and sold to employers to pay off never ending debt. Homeless addicts are also kept in peonage with growers using drug debts to make them accept slavery. Think about that when you drink your morning orange juice or eat your chicken (both of which are notorious for enslaving employees and using piece work to underpay employees).

Piecework even applies to garbage collectors, who are paid to do their routes, not by the hour. If middle-class workers were faced with such conditions, they would likely not take the job for the pay offered, if at all, unless they are desperate.

Immigration reform efforts are scuttled by employers who take advantage of the status quo. The last time they were one vote from passage, the issue of birth-right citizenship came up and Lindsey Graham got cold feet. The next session saw an immigration reform bill where a compromise was made in the Senate and sent to the House to be voted on, knowing that the vote would not come. Indeed, the bill was draconian. Passage would have laid onerous conditions on immigrants.

The real problem is the right-to-work laws which are really right-to-hire-the-undocumented laws. No one would hire an undocumented worker unless necessary if they had to pay union wages and adhere to work rules. Likewise, if there were no restrictions on hiring, workers would complain about pay and conditions, which would change who is hired. The same people might be, but they would no longer be slaves.

The market for wage slaves, like taxation and spending, yield unequal results.

It is deliberately designed that way and is news to absolutely no one. We accept these conditions, from the professional workforce (where the company demands patent rights and pays a pittance for them while the CEOs pocket the gains) to agricultural slave laborers, because we are told that There Is No Alternative. Marxists beg to differ. It is time to show how.

There is a Better Alternative

Jesus talked about depending on God and his followers created communism, and then became Stoic Hellenists. Marx talked about Socialism, rejected God and got a brotherhood and then State Capitalism. This is what happens when you ignore the details about the future. Marx talked in general about the automated worker's paradise. We are half way there, but only when it is cheaper than off-shore slavery.

Marx stated that in the future, the workers would figure things out democratically. As Michael Harrington noted in *Socialism: Past and Future*, even the Nordic

Social Democrats had no idea how to get to real Socialism. Democratic cooperatives have never grown to be significant.

Employee Stock Ownership Programs limit real ownership to a deal for the founders, possibly lower CEO pay and a monthly lecture on ownership culture with a plate of lasagna. The workers should adopt socialist answers democratically, but they need to be given the right questions. So, let's ask them. That is how we get to that Better Alternative.

First some concepts: We all know that the Socialist Ideal is that the Workers Control the Means of Production. The modern assumptions are that Voters Control the Means of Government, Management Controls the Means of Production and Consumers Control the Means of Consumption. The modern reality is that Capitalists Control the Means of Government, Production and Consumption. In Stalinism, Comrades Control the Means of Government, Production and Consumption. In a new culture of ownership, Employee-Owners control the Means of Consumption, Production and Government.

Governance and Rewards

Let us start with the most basic question, which applies more to new Enterprises to mature companies: How do Enterprises get revenue from outside? Do they have cash cows or do innovation and sell the intellectual property rights?

Employee- owned companies can decide who is in charge. Options include the current Board of Directors, a Board Representing Occupations with voting strength on a share or warm body basis or by a direct vote of members by all shares or one per member on a cooperative model.

There are two possible contexts for ownership: Workers can retain current hierarchical structures and reward systems or can adopt systems which match new ownership reality and reflect a new culture, which must be more egalitarian AND individualistic.

Is there profit (let's hope) and is it distributed only as dividends or as a dividend to reward capital (including employee-owned capital), as bonuses to innovators and the remainder according to salary or as above with remainder the distributed to each worker evenly.

Who does the Enterprise include as voters: 1099 Contract Employees Temporary employees? Franchise employees of their product? (ex., dealerships) Franchise employees as part of a larger cooperative in area serving them? (ex., Theater, Fast Food) Service workers? (Admin., Custodial). What about tenure? Immediate (Day One), Six Months or One Year? Is the Enterprise international? Are their workers our slaves or fellow members with an equal standard of living? What domestic and international industries are absorbed?

Who decides on rewards? Does everyone get equal rewards? Are they distributed by management or by work teams? Are disputes settled by share or member vote? What kind of rewards? Cash, higher salary (not recommended), shares (Dividends realized or reinvested) or some combination of cash and shares?

Who chooses the CEO? A unitary Board of Directors Representative Board? The lowest pre- qualified bidder with ties resoled by share vote or member vote? Who choses managers and supervisors? Higher management, peers, supervised employees by share or member, or does the job go to the lowest bidder.

Do members get higher pay for longevity and innovation or stock. What about funding retirement? Is it share based or an annuity or some combination of both after some percentage of shares are spent down or the member worker dies? Do retirees retain voting rights? Will they still participate in Social Security, if it is still offered?

How do Enterprises do affirmative action? Deny racism and sexism exists? Quotas? Random selection? How about super qualified candidates? Member advantages (i.e., legacies)? Do they employ low skilled workers then train them?

Does the Enterprise offer sick leave or paid vacations? Are there bonuses to go? Can members get paid flights and cars? Are there Coop time shares and restaurants? Do they or buy into existing providers or even become one? Are leave entitlements for newly hired senior workers grandfathered? Does leave accrue with experience or is it the same for everyone?

If there are unions is it an open or closed shop? This is a question where political activity may be required, either by each enterprise or an organization representing them. What is the Union role? Traditional/Adversarial? Do they represent

Franchise Employees (if that system is retained)? Are they Board Representatives? Are Unions and Associations an occupational voting bloc with decisions on a winner take all basis or divided by shares with factions or by member vote?

What does the Enterprise do about medical malpractice: disciple, lawsuits or arbitration? What does the Enterprise do with addicts or shopaholics or laggards? Can members be expelled and paid off? Does it try intervention first? What do they do about mental healthcare for extended family without insurance? Do they cover them or leave them to religious or government care?

What do Enterprises do with workers whose skills are obsolete? Is there unemployment insurance or are they funded with their own retirement shares? Are their mortgages held in abeyance while they look for another Enterprise? Are there best practices to be followed or does each cooperative or subunit self- govern?

Training and Education

How do enterprises offer vocational training and pay for it? Do parents pay, the government or the Enterprise, with hiring up front? Who pays for student living expenses and does training carry a service obligation and what to do if it does not work out? The same questions can be asked regarding the last two years of high school and junior college and for more advanced academic studies.

Do students and younger workers get subsidized or cooperative apartments, live on campus or just a salary high enough no to live in a group house? What about meals? Full board, breakfast and lunch with dinner out or an in-cooperative dining club (like officer's and NCO clubs?

How are workers at dining facilities paid? Are they also members with member salaries, contractors, second class citizens or work studies?

Does cooperative education lead to higher salaries or stock bonuses? How do we compensate older employees for education and invention while working toward equality or is the firm not ready for such radical solutions?

When do students or trainees become voting members who also accumulate preferred shares or are all shares voting so that experience has more of a say, and if so, how much more?

What about K-10 education? Can members choose to fund education in lieu of taxes or get free tuition at public, cooperative or parish schools? Who funds or delivers remedial education? Does the Enterprise? Should we try to find untapped genius? It is up to the workers and members to decide.

Cooperative Living

Ownership needs to be about what is on the menu in the cafeteria. It needs to first decide if there is one. Do people buy their food on their own or use cooperative stores? Is it free or purchased? Does the Enterprise allow workers to establish restaurants and are these open to public and is this food free or at a discount? What benefits are members only?

Do we include Enterprise owned farms staffed by voting members? Do housing options include in home habitats using the latest in space technology? Is animal husbandry included? What about meat or substitutes? Does excess go to a cooperative market or barter store? GMOs? Cloned meat?

What about housing for families and older workers? Do they rent or own. Does the Enterprise build or sell them or are members on their own? Does the enterprise purchase or build them? Do members use outside finance or is Enterprise provided? Is debt in cash or standard labor hours? Do members pay interest or is the cost of money taken it out of profit? Are there free upgrades for family size? Who owns the land? Individuals or land trusts? Who pays property taxes, individuals or the Enterprise?

Is there an in-house medical staff, including nurses, doctors, nursing assistants and specialists? How big is the firm in terms of medical workload and supporting medical education? What about daycare, including for sick kids?

Does the Enterprise self-insure and offer credit or go with outside products? Is this a group or individual decision? Are all services voluntary or are decisions democratic and results mandatory? How long is the work week? Flexible hours? Do members work a shorter day if they grow their own food?

In general, what do people wear to work? Uniforms, casual, business casual or semi-formal and who buys? In house or clothing allowance? All these are essentially make or buy decisions, including whether vendors are used or the workers are voting coop members. Do they offer non-work clothing?

What about water and trash recycling, composting and purification? Are these in home, cooperative or public? What about utilities?

Is road building and maintenance done individually using a Smart Growth system and is it shared with other cooperatives, including car manufacturers and energy companies? Are they grid? Do they use alternative energy? Are cars self-driving with central computer control? Are roads covered and use electric cars? Is there public transportation? Are there other self-generated options? How is it all financed? Is there debt and from whom? Is transportation free for all or just retirees? Do members own shares in each other's Enterprises? Do they vote them?

What about gasoline? Are there Enterprise gas stations or do we let big oil, Wall Street, banks and other outside finance die? Again, it is up to members what they make, what they buy and what to kill off. I certainly have an opinion on Big Oil. Can you guess what it is? How do we decide?

Politics

We decide by asking more questions. Should Enterprises work for Medicare for All, with or without optional care inside each Enterprise? Should they support status quo or work for change?

What does the sector do about both immigration and trade, or is this left to individual firms? What about imports, immigrants, the supply chain and transfer pricing? Do they buy out Russian and Chinese Party Oligarchs? Does the sector ferment revolution? What about Brahmanism in India?

Do international Enterprises assert extra-territoriality and protect themselves with armed or even armored guards against corrupt local government?

Do Enterprises sell weapons or even supplies to military? Do we take a principled stance and oppose all war?

Do Enterprises participate in space exploration as an alternative to building weapons, maybe even as a cash cow? A Mars cooperative? Do Enterprises use exploration research to improve our own habitat concepts?

Do Enterprises directly support reservists and veterans, especially with health care? Do we help take homeless veterans off the street? Are these services provided by cooperatives in lieu of taxes or contracted with the VA?

Does each Enterprise decide on its own what to do about leave and benefits or do all cooperatives decide as a group?

Do Enterprises make or buy entertainment or sports teams? Do Enterprises participate in high school or junior college football, community theater, cinema, with or without free popcorn? Are professional teams co-owned with cities who provide the venue? Are there alternative sports leagues or do they buy existing teams? How do they pay superstars? What about retired athletes? Do retirees vote their shares or trade them in? Do they include stadium workers in the Enterprise?

Do Enterprises support tax reform? Value added only or income taxes as well, at least to pay off debt and pay for debt financed military adventures? Do they support subtraction VATs channel family subsidies, education and social services with privatization alternatives?

Do Enterprises support land value taxes and citizens dividend or support outsiders in our midst with cooperative services?

What about the drive for ownership? Does it support insured personal accounts holding voting stock as a way to change the entire economy? Do we build political alliances to expand the system? Do we have one big coop or firms taking different positions?

What does the system do about business or cooperative failures? Is there insurance for members against failure? Can that insurance also be used to lend money to Enterprises rather than Wall Street?

Do coops decide on issues for themselves or practice Democratic centralism? What should they do about campaign contributions? Are cooperatives people too, including defeating capitalism?

Here is the question everyone is interested in: do we convert the economy using free market competition, with subsidies that can be rejected or do we impose this on society?

Further Reading

If you want to get into the nuts and bolts of Capitalism and Socialism and you really like to read complicated economic studies, there is nothing like the three volumes of Capital by Karl Marx and Friedrich Engels. There is also an audio book series.

If you want an explanation of what is in Capital and the arguments over it, as well as case studies about the issues in the 1970s and before regarding welfare, the history of Aramco in Saudi Arabia and the oil shocks, then the book to read is *The Twilight of Capitalism* by Michael Harrington, who also wrote the classic history of *Socialism: Past and Future.*

For a concise primer on *Capital*, Richard Wolff just released the pamphlet Understanding Marxism. He also wrote *Democracy at Work: A Cure for Capitalism.*

Aside from the original Marx, I have reviewed all of these works in my web pages xianleft.blogspot.com, Fiscalequity.blogspot.com and BindnerAnalytics.blogspot.com. All but *The Twilight* are also included in my deeper treatment of cooperative socialism, The Future Is Calling: It Wants Your Stuff. Enjoy. Consider it socialist binge reading.